BRIGHT IDEA BOOKS

SPOOKY Folktales

by Blake Hoena

CAPSTONE PRESS
a capstone imprint

Bright Idea Books are published by Capstone Press
1710 Roe Crest Drive, North Mankato, Minnesota 56003
www.mycapstone.com

Library of Congress Cataloging-in-Publication Data
Names: Hoena, B. A., author.
Title: Spooky folktales / by Blake Hoena.
Description: North Mankato : Capstone Press, 2019. | Series: Ghosts and hauntings | Includes bibliographical references and index.
Identifiers: LCCN 2018018694 (print) | LCCN 2018024483 (ebook) | ISBN 9781543541915 (ebook) | ISBN 9781543541519 (hardcover : alk. paper)
Subjects: LCSH: Ghosts. | Tales.
Classification: LCC BF1461 (ebook) | LCC BF1461 .H575 2019 (print) | DDC 133.1--dc23
LC record available at https://lccn.loc.gov/2018018694

Editorial Credits
Editor: Alexis Burling
Designer: Becky Daum
Production Specialist: Colleen McLaren

Photo Credits
Glow Images: Fine Art Images/Heritage Images, 26–27; iStockphoto: BernardAllum, 22–23, 24, ehrlif, 12–13, Mimadeo, 8–9; Shutterstock Images: adike, 5, Alexandra Lande, cover (background), Alina G, 30–31, Emeryk III, 18–19, FOTOKITA, 11, 28, Ilkin Zeferli, 6–7, jurgenfr, cover (foreground), Nomad_Soul, 14, Oleh flyagulaka, 17, tatui suwat, 20–21

Design Elements: iStockphoto, Red Line Editorial, and Shutterstock Images

Printed and bound in the USA. PO5847

TABLE OF CONTENTS

CHAPTER 1

CALL OF THE Nishi Dak

Have you ever imagined that animals could talk? Did you ever wish that magic was real? Have you wanted to battle a giant? All of those things are parts of folktales.

Folktales are **traditional** stories. They come from people's imaginations. These stories are often shared **orally**. People pass the stories down by telling them to others over many years.

Dragons are a big part of folktales in many cultures.

Dark rooms are said to be hiding places for Nishi Dak.

Some ghost stories are folktales. One folktale comes from West Bengal in India. People there are told to beware of strange sounds at night. It might be a Nishi Dak.

Nishi Dak are the **spirits** of people who died. The people did not have proper burials. Nishi Dak come out when it is dark. They appear as distant shadows.

CALL OF THE NIGHT

Nishi means "night." *Dak* or *Daak* means "call." So *Nishi Dak* means "call of the night."

Nishi Dak are said to lure their victims into dark forests.

A person might hear a voice they know. It could sound like a friend or family member. But it is not safe to follow the voice. It could be a Nishi Dak.

Nishi Dak try to lead people into dark alleys or other spooky places. The people get lost. They are never seen again.

Stories say Nishi Dak cannot call out more than twice. People should wait to hear their name three times. Then they will know they are safe.

CHAPTER 2

GHOST-WITCH

In some folktales the dead do not stay dead. That is true in Wabanaki stories. These American Indians have tales about the *skadegamutc* (skuh-da-goo-much).

A skadegamutc is a ghost-witch. The witch is dead and comes back to life. During the day it appears as a **corpse**. At night it seeks out victims.

The skadegamutc rises from the dead as soon as the sun goes down.

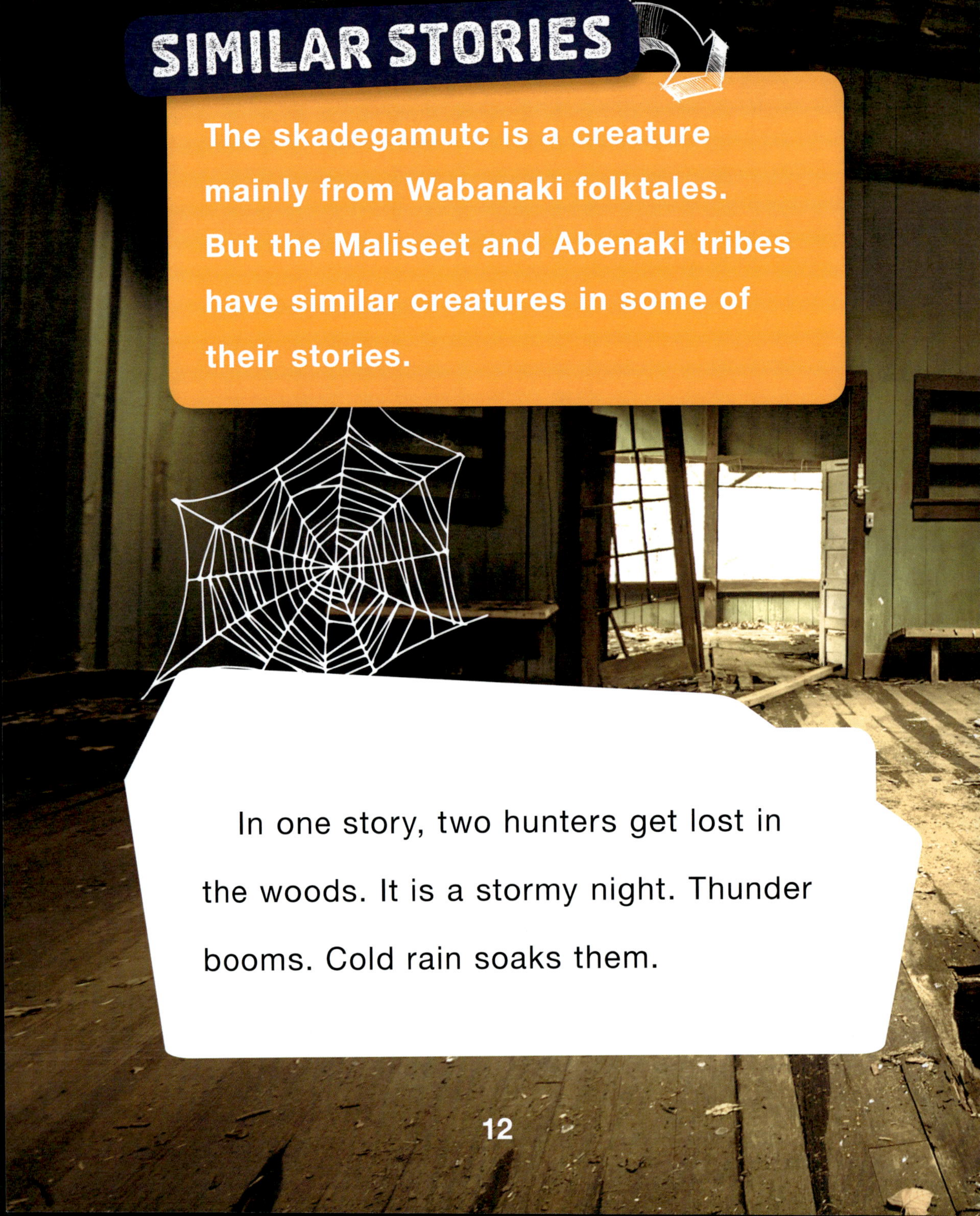

SIMILAR STORIES

The skadegamutc is a creature mainly from Wabanaki folktales. But the Maliseet and Abenaki tribes have similar creatures in some of their stories.

In one story, two hunters get lost in the woods. It is a stormy night. Thunder booms. Cold rain soaks them.

The hunters need shelter. They find a cabin. A dead body lies in one corner. But the hunters stay anyway because of the storm.

The cabin is falling apart. But it keeps the hunters dry.

A skadegamutc looks very similar to a zombie.

The hunters start a fire. They cook a meal. Then they go to sleep.

That night one hunter is awakened. He hears **gurgling** noises. He turns to his friend. What he sees horrifies him. The dead body is a skadegamutc! It is sucking the blood from his friend. The remaining hunter runs for his life.

CHAPTER 3

HUMAN-EATING Biloko

Biloko are human-eating ghosts in folktales from Africa. They are said to **haunt** the forests there. Biloko have razor-sharp teeth and claws. They can open their mouths wide enough to swallow a person whole.

Forest monsters are common in folktales.

Biloko like to strike at night.

A popular folktale starts with a man going off to hunt. His wife stays home. That night she hears a strange noise. It sounds like a bell. She opens the door of her hut. In front of her stands a kind of Biloko called an Eloko.

The bell sound puts the woman under a **spell**. She asks the Eloko if it is hungry. It says it only eats human flesh. She holds out her arm. The Eloko takes a bite!

Later that night the hunter returns home. All he finds is his wife's bones.

After eating human flesh, the Eloko leaves a pile of bones behind.

CHAPTER 4

THE PEONY Lantern

One of the most famous folktales in Japan is called "The **Peony** Lantern." It is about a samurai named Ogiwara Shinnojo. Samurai were Japanese warriors.

Samurai fought with sharp swords.

One night Ogiwara sits on his porch. He feels sad and lonely. His wife has just died. He does not know if he will find love again.

Otsuyu and the maid are dressed in robes made of beautiful fabric.

Then he sees a glowing light. It is a maid. She carries a lantern. The lantern has the symbol of a peony on it.

A beautiful woman is with the maid. The woman's name is Otsuyu. Ogiwara and Otsuyu fall in love. They meet at night. Ogiwara sleeps during the day.

LUCKY FLOWERS

Peonies are often seen as symbols of love. In Japanese stories they also represent good luck.

A neighbor is worried about Ogiwara. So he goes to visit one night. What he sees terrifies him. He does not see Ogiwara with a beautiful woman. He sees Otsuyu as a rotting corpse. Ogiwara is in love with a ghost!

The townspeople tell Ogiwara he is in danger. But he is under Otsuyu's spell. He will not listen to them.

Then Ogiwara disappears. People search for him. They see a **crypt** in the graveyard. The name Otsuyu is on it. Otsuyu's maid is also buried there.

Japanese folklore has many scary stories. They tell about ghosts and evil spirits.

The people search the crypt. There is something horrifying inside. Ogiwara is dead. A look of fear is on his face. Otsuyu's corpse is wrapped around his body.

GLOSSARY

corpse
the body of a dead person

crypt
a chamber, often underground, where the dead are buried

gurgling
a bubbling sound

haunt
to visit as a ghost

orally
having to do with speech

peony
a type of flowering plant

spell
a spoken word or words that have magic powers

spirits
ghosts

traditional
based on the customs of a group of people

TRIVIA

1. Cultures as far back as the ancient Sumerians in 4000 BC believed in ghosts. These spirits were said to haunt people who were still alive.

2. There are many kinds of folktales. Animal tales have talking animals. Wonder tales use magic. *Pourquoi* tales explain how something came to be. The word *pourquoi* means "why" in French.

3. Jacob and Wilhelm Grimm gathered one of the best-known collections of folktales. *Kinder und Hausmärchen*, or *Children's and Household Tales*, was published in 1812. It contains more than 200 stories. Many of the stories are scary.

ACTIVITY

Now it is time to write your own ghostly folktale. Sometimes folktales were people's attempts to explain things they did not understand. It could be the source of scary noises or strange shapes in the night.

Write down what scares you. Then imagine what type of ghost or creature might cause this scary thing. Now write your folktale.

You will need to describe the setting. Most ghosts haunt a certain place. Add in details as you write. Is the ghost helpful or harmful? How does the ghost cause the thing that scares you? What happens to people who meet the ghost?

When you are done writing, share your story with friends.

FURTHER RESOURCES

Fascinated by folktales? Read even more folktales in this book:

Randolph, Joanne. *Early American Legends and Folktales*. New York: Cavendish Square Publishing, 2018.

Ready to find out more about folktales in different parts of the world? Check out these websites:

American Folklore
http://americanfolklore.net

Anike Foundation: African Folktales
http://anikefoundation.org/index.php/african-folktales/

Native American Indian Legends and Folklore
http://www.native-languages.org/legends.htm

Telling Tales from Southeast Asia and Korea
http://asianfolktales.unescoapceiu.org/sub2.htm

INDEX